Gaming Beyond Entertainment:
The Social and Cultural Impact of Video Games

By

Andrew A. Headley

Gaming Beyond Entertainment:
The Social and Cultural Impact of Video Games

Gaming Beyond Entertainment:
The Social and Cultural Impact of Video Games

TABLE OF CONTENTS

CHAPTER I
Introduction

A. The Rise of Video Games

In the modern era, few phenomena have had as profound an impact on entertainment and culture as the rise of video games. What began as simple, pixelated amusements in arcades has blossomed into a multi-billion-dollar industry that spans the globe, captivating people of all ages and backgrounds. Video games have evolved from humble beginnings into a cultural force that extends far beyond mere entertainment, influencing society in unexpected and far-reaching ways.

The journey of video games traces back to the mid-20th century when academics and scientists dabbled with interactive computer simulations. However, it was not until the early 1970s that video games made their grand entrance into mainstream culture. The game "Pong," with its primitive graphics and straightforward gameplay, introduced the world to a new form of amusement that quickly gained popularity in arcades and homes alike.

This pioneering game laid the groundwork for the extraordinary evolution of the gaming industry.

As technology advanced, so too did the complexity and diversity of video games. The 1980s marked a golden era for gaming, with the introduction of iconic titles such as "Super Mario Bros," "Tetris," and "The Legend of Zelda." These games not only revolutionized the industry but also embedded themselves in the collective consciousness of millions, creating lifelong enthusiasts.

The emergence of personal computers in the 1990s further expanded the horizons of gaming. Gaming developers began crafting intricate narratives and more immersive worlds, opening up new avenues for storytelling and player engagement. Adventure and role-playing games like "Final Fantasy" and "Myst" captured the imaginations of players, offering them a chance to embark on epic quests and emotionally-charged adventures.

However, the most significant leap forward in gaming came with the rapid evolution of consoles and the advent of the internet in the late 1990s and early 2000s. Online gaming took center stage, enabling players to connect and compete with others worldwide. This connectivity not only transformed gaming into a social activity but also laid the groundwork for the formation of virtual communities.

With the rise of multiplayer online games, such as "World of Warcraft" and "Counter-Strike," players could forge friendships, alliances, and rivalries with individuals they might never meet in person. The virtual realm became a place of belonging, offering a sense of identity and camaraderie that transcended geographical boundaries.

Furthermore, the growth of mobile gaming in the last decade has made video games even more accessible to a global audience. From casual puzzle games to complex strategy titles, the diverse range of mobile gaming experiences has solidified gaming's position as a ubiquitous form of entertainment and communication.

As video games continue to advance, they have become intertwined with various aspects of modern life. They have infiltrated education, with educators recognizing their potential as engaging tools for learning and skill development. Additionally, video games have made their way into the arts, influencing music, film, and literature, and even inspiring new forms of artistic expression.

Beyond entertainment, video games have also emerged as an economic powerhouse, spawning competitive esports leagues and professional gaming careers. Esports events now attract massive audiences, rivaling traditional sports in terms of viewership and sponsorship.

The rise of video games is not without its controversies and challenges, however. Concerns have been raised about the potential negative effects of excessive gaming, including addiction and social isolation. Moreover, the industry has faced scrutiny over issues of representation, diversity, and gender inclusivity in game development and narratives.

In conclusion, the ascent of video games from humble origins to a global cultural phenomenon is a testament to their enduring appeal and societal impact. This book delves into the social and cultural significance of video games, exploring their role in shaping our interactions, perceptions, and collective identity. As we embark on this journey through the world of gaming, we aim to uncover the profound influence video games have had and continue to have on our lives and the world at large.

B. The Evolution of Gaming Culture

Video games have come a long way since their humble beginnings, not just in terms of technological advancements but also in the way they have shaped and evolved gaming culture. What started as a niche hobby for a few enthusiasts has blossomed into a global phenomenon, intertwining with various aspects of modern life. The evolution of gaming culture reflects the changing attitudes and perceptions surrounding video games, transforming them from mere entertainment to a powerful force that influences social interactions, identity, and even artistic expression.

In the early days of gaming, the culture revolved around arcade halls and local gatherings. Gamers would flock to these physical spaces to challenge their skills, exchange tips, and engage in friendly competition. The sense of community among players was fostered through face-to-face interactions, creating a unique camaraderie among gaming enthusiasts.

With the advent of home gaming consoles and personal computers, gaming culture underwent a significant shift. Players could now enjoy games from the comfort of their homes, enabling more extended gameplay sessions and the rise of single-player experiences. Iconic gaming consoles like the Nintendo Entertainment System (NES) and Sega Genesis paved the way for memorable gaming experiences that resonated with players of all ages.

As technology progressed, so did the opportunities for multiplayer gaming experiences. The birth of online gaming introduced an entirely new dimension to gaming culture, revolutionizing the way people interacted with games and each other. Multiplayer games allowed players from across the world to connect and collaborate, transcending geographical barriers and fostering diverse virtual communities. Online forums and chat platforms emerged, serving as virtual meeting places where players could share their passion for gaming and discuss strategies.

The social aspect of gaming culture was further amplified by the rise of social media. Platforms like Twitch and YouTube gave birth to a new breed of gaming celebrities and content creators. Gamers could now share their experiences, skills, and humor with vast audiences, transforming gaming into a form of entertainment not only for players but also for spectators. Esports events, featuring professional gamers competing on a global stage, drew massive crowds both in-person and online, legitimizing gaming as a mainstream spectator sport.

Gaming culture has also had a profound impact on broader pop culture. Video game characters, stories, and memes have become ingrained in society's collective consciousness. Gamers find inspiration from their favorite games, creating fan art, fan fiction, and incorporating gaming elements into other art forms. This fusion of gaming with music, movies, and literature has given rise to a rich tapestry of cultural crossovers that continuously evolve and influence each other.

The inclusive nature of gaming culture has also played a crucial role in breaking down barriers and promoting diversity. Gaming has become a haven where individuals from diverse backgrounds can come together, transcending differences and connecting over shared passions. Video games have become a medium through which marginalized voices can be heard, as developers and players alike seek to create more inclusive and representative gaming experiences.

However, as gaming culture has grown, it has not been without challenges. Issues of toxicity, harassment, and discrimination have marred the online gaming landscape, highlighting the need for creating safer and more welcoming spaces for players. The industry has had to confront these challenges head-on, striving to establish a culture that promotes respect, inclusivity, and fair play.

In this book, we explore the rich tapestry of gaming culture, tracing its evolution from its roots in arcades to the expansive global phenomenon it is today. We delve into the social and cultural implications of gaming, analyzing how video games have influenced our society, communication, and sense of identity. As we embark on this journey, we aim to shed light on the transformative power of gaming culture and the profound ways it continues to shape the world we live in.

C. Purpose and Scope of the Book

Video games have emerged as a cultural and social force that goes beyond mere entertainment. Their influence reaches into various aspects of modern life, shaping how we interact, learn, and perceive the world around us. This book, "Gaming Beyond Entertainment: The Social and Cultural Impact of Video Games," aims to delve into the profound and multifaceted effects of video games on society, providing a comprehensive exploration of their significance and potential.

Purpose of the Book:

The primary purpose of this book is to analyze and showcase the extensive impact of video games beyond their traditional role as entertainment. While gaming has long been associated with leisure and escapism, it is crucial to recognize that video games have evolved into an influential cultural medium with far-reaching consequences. Through rigorous research, case studies, and expert insights, this book aims to shed light on the ways video games have transformed social dynamics, educational paradigms, artistic expression, and cultural values.

As a diverse and dynamic field, gaming culture warrants in-depth examination, and this book seeks to bridge the gap between academic analysis and general awareness. While academic research has explored various aspects of gaming's impact, its insights often remain confined within specialized circles. This book strives to make this valuable knowledge accessible to a broader audience, including gamers, educators, policymakers, and anyone interested in understanding the broader implications of video games.

Scope of the Book:

The scope of this book is comprehensive, spanning across diverse dimensions of the social and cultural impact of video games. It covers a wide range of topics, each contributing to a holistic understanding of gaming's influence on society.

The book explores the social impact of video games, delving into the ways they have become more than just a solitary pastime. It examines how online gaming communities have fostered a sense of belonging and camaraderie among players worldwide. Additionally, it delves into the positive effects of video games on social skills development, such as teamwork, communication, empathy, and emotional intelligence. Furthermore, the book addresses video games' role in addressing social issues, including representation, diversity, and even their potential in advocating for social causes.

Culturally, video games have become an integral part of our artistic expression and heritage. This book analyzes how video games have evolved into cultural artifacts that reflect and reshape our collective identity. It investigates how video games portray and challenge cultural stereotypes, and how they can contribute to cultural preservation by reviving folklore and traditions.

Moreover, the book explores the educational potential of video games, highlighting how they can be utilized for gamified learning, serious educational purposes, and cognitive skill development. It examines the opportunities and challenges of integrating video games into formal education systems.

Mental health is another significant area addressed in the book. It delves into the psychology of gaming, examining both the potential benefits and risks, including gaming addiction and its impact on psychological well-being. Moreover, it showcases how video games can serve as therapeutic tools, aiding in stress management and mental health treatment.

The book also examines emerging trends in gaming, including virtual reality and augmented reality, and their potential social and ethical implications. It explores the rise of esports and its influence on traditional sports and society, as well as the role of gaming in driving social change and fostering social movements.

In conclusion, "Gaming Beyond Entertainment: The Social and Cultural Impact of Video Games" sets out to provide a comprehensive and enlightening exploration of the profound influence video games have on society and culture. By examining the multifaceted dimensions of gaming's impact, the book aims to foster a deeper understanding of this dynamic medium and its transformative power in shaping the world we live in.

CHAPTER II
Exploring the Social Impact of Video Games

A. Video Games as a Social Platform

In recent years, video games have evolved beyond being solitary experiences and have become robust social platforms, enabling players from around the globe to connect, collaborate, and form meaningful relationships. The social aspect of gaming has transformed the way people interact, forging new friendships and virtual communities that transcend physical boundaries.

1. Online Gaming Communities:

One of the most significant developments in gaming culture has been the rise of online gaming communities. With the advent of high-speed internet and advanced networking technologies, players can now join vast virtual realms where they interact with others in real-time. These communities are not only spaces for gaming but also serve as digital meeting grounds where people with shared interests converge.

Massively multiplayer online games (MMOs) like "World of Warcraft" and "Guild Wars 2" exemplify the power of online gaming communities. In these virtual worlds, players collaborate on quests, form guilds, and strategize to conquer challenges. The relationships forged within these games can be enduring, transcending the boundaries of the virtual realm. Many players develop genuine friendships with people they may have never met face-to-face.

Moreover, online gaming communities offer a haven for individuals who might otherwise feel socially isolated or marginalized. In these digital spaces, players can find a sense of belonging, acceptance, and camaraderie, regardless of their real-world circumstances. This inclusive nature of gaming communities has been a source of empowerment for many, allowing them to express themselves freely without fear of judgment.

However, the rise of online gaming communities has also brought forth challenges. Toxic behavior and harassment within these spaces can undermine the positive social experience. Game developers and platform providers have been striving to implement measures to promote healthy and respectful interactions within gaming communities. Initiatives such as reporting systems, player moderation, and community guidelines are being used to foster a safe and enjoyable social environment for all players.

2. Virtual Reality and Social Interaction:

The advent of virtual reality (VR) has taken the social aspect of gaming to new heights. VR allows players to immerse themselves in realistic, three-dimensional environments, creating a sense of presence and shared experiences. VR social platforms and multiplayer games offer a level of interaction previously unimaginable in traditional gaming.

Social VR platforms like "VRChat" and "AltspaceVR" enable users to meet and socialize with others in virtual spaces. Avatars represent players, and they can communicate through voice chat or gestures, fostering a sense of presence and social connection. These platforms facilitate virtual meetups, allowing people from different parts of the world to interact as if they were in the same physical location.

VR gaming experiences, such as cooperative missions or sports simulations, emphasize teamwork and cooperation. Players must communicate effectively to achieve their objectives, leading to the formation of strong bonds among teammates. The social nature of these experiences often extends beyond the virtual realm, as players may organize meetups or maintain contact through other means outside the VR space.

Virtual reality has also been a powerful tool for individuals with physical disabilities or mobility constraints, providing them with opportunities for social interaction and experiences that might otherwise be inaccessible. Through VR, they can participate in activities and social events, breaking down barriers and promoting inclusivity.

However, as VR becomes more prevalent, ethical considerations emerge. Issues such as privacy, consent, and the potential for virtual harassment need careful attention. Developers and platform providers must prioritize user safety and ensure that VR spaces remain welcoming and respectful environments.

In conclusion, video games have evolved into vibrant social platforms that facilitate meaningful connections and interactions among players. Online gaming communities offer a sense of belonging and camaraderie, transcending geographical barriers. Virtual reality enhances social experiences, providing a sense of presence and shared activities. As technology continues to advance, the social impact of video games is likely to grow, shaping how people connect and build relationships in both virtual and real-world settings.

B. Video Games and Social Skills Development

While video games are often criticized for promoting isolation, research has revealed that gaming can actually have a positive impact on social skills development. As players engage in various gaming experiences, they encounter opportunities to communicate, collaborate, and navigate complex social dynamics. This section delves into two essential aspects of social skills development through video games: communication and teamwork, and empathy and emotional intelligence.

1. Communication and Teamwork:

Effective communication and teamwork are essential skills in both virtual and real-world settings, and video games provide a unique environment for honing these abilities. Many modern games, particularly multiplayer ones, require players to collaborate to achieve shared objectives. This necessitates effective communication to strategize, coordinate actions, and adapt to rapidly changing situations.

Team-based competitive games like "Overwatch" and "League of Legends" exemplify the significance of communication and teamwork. Players must communicate vital information, such as enemy positions or resource management, to gain a competitive advantage. As they work together towards a common goal, they learn to trust each other's abilities and rely on effective communication to succeed.

Moreover, gaming often brings together individuals from diverse backgrounds and cultures. In these multicultural gaming environments, players are exposed to different communication styles and cultural norms. This exposure fosters cross-cultural understanding, empathy, and appreciation for diversity.

Beyond multiplayer games, single-player experiences can also contribute to social skills development. Narrative-driven games often present players with choices that impact the story and characters. These choices require players to empathize with virtual characters and consider the consequences of their actions, nurturing emotional intelligence and moral reasoning.

2. Empathy and Emotional Intelligence:

Empathy, the ability to understand and share the feelings of others, is a crucial aspect of social skills development. Video games can facilitate the cultivation of empathy by immersing players in emotionally rich narratives and allowing them to inhabit the perspectives of characters with diverse experiences.

Games like "Life is Strange" and "The Last of Us" feature deep, character-driven storytelling that prompts players to empathize with the struggles, joys, and sorrows of virtual protagonists. By emotionally investing in these characters' journeys, players develop a heightened sense of empathy and compassion, which can transfer to their real-world interactions.

Furthermore, video games often present players with moral dilemmas and ethical choices. Players must grapple with these situations, weighing the consequences of their decisions on in-game characters and the game world. This process cultivates emotional intelligence, as players learn to navigate complex emotions and consider the impact of their actions on others.

Games with multiplayer interactions also foster empathy by exposing players to the feelings and perspectives of their fellow gamers. Experiencing triumphs and setbacks together creates an emotional connection and a shared sense of camaraderie, encouraging players to be supportive and understanding of one another.

While video games can positively contribute to social skills development, it is essential to strike a balance. Excessive gaming without real-world social interactions can lead to isolation and hinder the development of essential face-to-face communication skills. However, when integrated mindfully into a balanced lifestyle, video games can serve as a valuable tool for strengthening social competencies.

In conclusion, video games offer a unique and engaging platform for developing vital social skills. Through teamwork and communication in multiplayer games, players enhance their ability to collaborate effectively with others. Immersive narratives and moral choices promote empathy and emotional intelligence, fostering understanding and compassion for virtual characters and, by extension, real-world individuals. As gaming continues to evolve, its potential to contribute positively to social skills development makes it a compelling medium for personal growth and social enrichment.

C. Video Games and Social Issues

Video games have emerged as a powerful platform for addressing and reflecting on a wide range of social issues. As an interactive medium, they offer opportunities for exploration, empathy, and education. This section examines how video games have influenced conversations surrounding representation and diversity, as well as their role in promoting social activism and driving positive change.

1. Representation and Diversity:

Historically, video games have been criticized for their lack of diverse and inclusive representation, particularly concerning gender, race, ethnicity, and sexual orientation. Many early games featured stereotypical or underrepresented characters, perpetuating harmful norms and limiting the potential for players to see themselves reflected in virtual worlds.

However, in recent years, the gaming industry has made strides in addressing these issues. Game developers and communities have advocated for more diverse representation, leading to the inclusion of a broader range of characters and stories. Games like "The Last of Us Part II" and "Life is Strange: True Colors" feature complex and diverse protagonists, providing players with a more inclusive gaming experience.

Moreover, character customization options in games like "The Sims" and "Mass Effect" allow players to create avatars that reflect their own identities, fostering a sense of personal representation and agency within virtual worlds. These inclusive practices not only promote empathy and understanding among players but also send a powerful message about the value of diversity in society.

Additionally, the representation of historical events and cultures in video games has also sparked discussions about cultural accuracy and authenticity. Games that explore historical settings, such as "Assassin's Creed" and "Ghost of Tsushima," have faced scrutiny for their portrayals of past events and cultures. This scrutiny has prompted developers to engage in more thoughtful research and consultation with relevant communities, striving for accurate and respectful representations.

2. Gaming and Social Activism:

Video games have the potential to be more than just entertainment; they can serve as a medium for social activism and advocacy. Game developers and players have leveraged gaming to shed light on critical social issues and encourage positive change in the real world.

Serious games, also known as social impact games, are explicitly designed to address social issues and educate players about real-world challenges. These games tackle topics such as environmental conservation, public health, and human rights. For example, "Papers, Please" confronts players with ethical dilemmas faced by immigration officers, challenging them to make decisions that reflect moral integrity and compassion.

Furthermore, video game communities have demonstrated their capacity for social activism. Players have united in support of causes, organizing in-game events or fundraisers to raise awareness and funds for various charitable organizations. For instance, gaming marathons, like "Games Done Quick," have raised millions of dollars for charities like Doctors Without Borders and the Prevent Cancer Foundation.

Gaming has also been used as a means of protest and resistance in regions experiencing social and political upheaval. During political movements, such as the Arab Spring and the Hong Kong protests, video games served as platforms for expressing dissent and solidarity. Gamers created in-game art and levels to reflect their aspirations for social change and to spread awareness on an international scale.

However, it is essential to recognize that not all social activism within gaming has been positively received. Some gaming communities have experienced backlash from individuals who prefer games to remain apolitical. This tension raises important questions about the boundaries of activism within gaming spaces and the role of creators and players in expressing political views.

In conclusion, video games have become an influential medium for addressing social issues and promoting social change. The push for more diverse representation in gaming reflects the industry's growing commitment to inclusivity and representation. Social impact games and gaming-related activism demonstrate how the gaming community can contribute positively to real-world causes and engage in social issues on a global scale. As video games continue to evolve, their potential as a catalyst for social awareness and activism remains an essential aspect of their social impact.

CHAPTER III
Investigating the Cultural Influence of Video Games

A. Video Games as Cultural Artifacts

Video games have emerged as a unique form of cultural expression, blending technology, storytelling, and interactive experiences into an art form that resonates with millions worldwide. This section explores the cultural significance of video games as artifacts that reflect and shape our collective identity. It delves into gaming as a form of expression and its relationship with storytelling traditions.

1. Gaming as a Form of Expression:

Just like literature, music, and cinema, video games have evolved into a powerful medium for creative expression. Game developers, designers, and artists use their craft to convey emotions, ideas, and narratives, allowing players to immerse themselves in interactive worlds that provoke thought and evoke emotions.

The artistry in video games can be seen in the visual design, music, and narrative elements. From breathtaking landscapes in open-world games like "The Legend of Zelda: Breath of the Wild" to emotionally charged musical compositions in games like "Journey," the artistic aspects of video games enrich the overall experience and elevate them to the status of cultural artifacts.

Furthermore, video games often tackle complex themes and explore philosophical questions, making players question their beliefs and values. Games like "Undertale" challenge traditional video game conventions and confront players with moral dilemmas, forcing them to contemplate the consequences of their actions. Through interactive storytelling, games can engage players on a profound emotional and intellectual level.

Gaming as a form of expression extends beyond the content of the games themselves. Player-created content, such as mods and fan art, also contributes to gaming culture as a form of creative expression. The communities that grow around popular games foster a vibrant ecosystem of fan-generated content, reflecting the shared passion and creativity of players.

2. Video Games and Storytelling Traditions:

Storytelling is an integral part of human culture, with traditions passed down through generations. Video games, as a storytelling medium, draw inspiration from these age-old traditions while also introducing innovative narrative techniques.

Narrative-driven games like "The Witcher 3: Wild Hunt" and "Red Dead Redemption 2" showcase the depth and complexity of storytelling in video games. Players become invested in the fates of well-developed characters, exploring intricate plotlines that rival those found in literature and film. The interactivity of games offers players agency, allowing them to shape the story's outcome based on their choices, blurring the line between authorship and audience.

Additionally, video games often draw inspiration from mythologies, folklore, and classic literature. Games like "God of War" draw from Greek mythology, "Okami" embraces Japanese folklore, and "Bioshock" explores philosophical concepts inspired by Ayn Rand's works. These references to cultural narratives add depth and meaning to gaming experiences, making them both engaging and intellectually stimulating.

Moreover, video games can also serve as a means of cultural preservation. Games that explore historical settings, such as the "Assassin's Creed" series, provide opportunities for players to learn about different time periods and cultures. These games often feature extensive historical research and attention to architectural and cultural details, contributing to a more immersive and educational experience.

The fusion of storytelling traditions with interactive gameplay creates a distinct narrative experience that distinguishes video games as a unique and potent cultural form. This blending of traditional storytelling with modern technology has opened up new frontiers for artistic expression, shaping the evolution of cultural narratives in the digital age.

In conclusion, video games have emerged as cultural artifacts that reflect and contribute to our collective identity. The artistic expression found in gaming, from visual design to narrative complexity, elevates video games to the status of an art form. The incorporation of storytelling traditions, along with innovative interactive elements, results in unique narrative experiences that engage players on multiple levels. As video games continue to evolve, they leave an indelible mark on our cultural landscape, inspiring creativity, exploration, and reflection within an ever-expanding gaming community.

B. Cultural Stereotypes in Video Games

As a form of media and cultural expression, video games have not been exempt from perpetuating cultural stereotypes. This section delves into the presence of cultural representations in video games and their potential impact on global perceptions. By examining how games portray different cultures, we can better understand the complexities of cultural representation in this evolving medium.

1. Examining Cultural Representations:

Video games often draw inspiration from various cultures around the world to create immersive and diverse virtual worlds. However, the portrayal of cultures in games can sometimes be oversimplified or based on stereotypes, leading to misconceptions and reinforcing biased beliefs.

One common example is the portrayal of Eastern cultures in Western-developed games. Some games set in Asia may depict characters and settings through a Western lens, leading to misrepresentations of cultural norms and practices. These portrayals might lack nuance and overlook the richness and diversity of Asian cultures.

Conversely, games developed in Eastern countries may also reinforce stereotypes about the West. Western characters in these games might be depicted as loud, aggressive, or ethnocentric, perpetuating cultural generalizations.

In addition to regional stereotypes, video games have occasionally featured racial and ethnic stereotypes. Characters from different ethnic backgrounds might be depicted with exaggerated physical features or assigned stereotypical roles, which can perpetuate harmful biases and misunderstandings.

Recognizing and addressing cultural stereotypes in video games is essential for fostering a more inclusive and respectful gaming culture. Game developers and storytellers have a responsibility to conduct thorough research and engage with diverse perspectives to create authentic and nuanced portrayals of cultures.

2. Impact on Global Perceptions:

Video games have a vast global reach, making them a powerful tool for shaping perceptions of different cultures. When players are exposed to cultural stereotypes in games, it can influence their perceptions of real-world cultures, leading to potentially harmful consequences.

For instance, if a video game portrays a specific culture as primitive or violent, players may internalize these stereotypes and develop biased views about people from that culture. This can reinforce harmful prejudices and perpetuate harmful attitudes towards individuals from those backgrounds.

Moreover, the global nature of the gaming community means that cultural stereotypes in games can have far-reaching effects. When games with stereotypical portrayals are distributed globally, they can reinforce existing biases and contribute to the spread of misinformation about cultures.

However, video games also have the potential to break down cultural barriers and foster understanding between players from different backgrounds. Games that present diverse and authentic cultural representations can promote empathy and curiosity about different cultures. By engaging players in narratives that challenge stereotypes and humanize characters from various backgrounds, video games can contribute to a more inclusive and tolerant society.

As the gaming industry continues to grow, game developers have increasingly recognized the importance of cultural sensitivity and accuracy. Many game studios are now actively working with cultural consultants and sensitivity readers to ensure that their games portray diverse cultures respectfully and authentically.

In conclusion, video games hold the power to influence global perceptions of cultures, both positively and negatively. While some games may perpetuate harmful stereotypes, there is a growing awareness within the industry about the importance of authentic and respectful cultural representations. By challenging cultural stereotypes and promoting diverse perspectives, video games can contribute to a more inclusive and understanding society. It is essential for developers and players alike to critically examine the portrayal of cultures in games, striving for greater cultural awareness and sensitivity in this evolving medium.

C. Video Games and Cultural Preservation

Video games have emerged as a powerful medium for preserving and reviving cultural heritage. This section explores how video games contribute to the preservation of folklore, myths, and cultural heritage. By incorporating traditional elements into gaming narratives and virtual worlds, video games play a significant role in keeping cultural legacies alive.

1. Revival of Folklore and Myths:

Folklore and myths are integral parts of cultural heritage, passing down stories, beliefs, and values from one generation to the next. Video games provide a unique opportunity to revive these ancient tales, allowing players to interact with legendary characters and explore fantastical realms inspired by folklore.

Games like "God of War" draw upon ancient Greek mythology, immersing players in a world of gods, monsters, and epic quests. By weaving the rich tapestry of Greek myths into its narrative, the game introduces players to legendary figures such as Zeus, Poseidon, and Kratos, while also exploring themes of hubris and fate. This fusion of classical mythology with interactive storytelling breathes new life into ancient tales and introduces them to younger audiences.

Similarly, "Ōkami" draws inspiration from Japanese folklore and Shinto beliefs. The game's protagonist, Amaterasu, embodies the sun goddess in the form of a wolf. As players embark on this artistic adventure, they encounter creatures and stories deeply rooted in Japanese tradition. "Ōkami" showcases the enduring appeal of folklore and demonstrates how video games can celebrate cultural heritage.

Video games also provide an opportunity to preserve lesser-known folklore and myths from various cultures that might not receive as much attention in mainstream media. By showcasing these lesser-known stories, games promote cultural diversity and appreciation for the vastness of human storytelling.

2. Cultural Heritage in Gaming:

Beyond folklore and myths, video games frequently incorporate elements of cultural heritage, including historical settings, architecture, and traditions. Games that meticulously recreate historical periods serve as virtual time capsules, transporting players to bygone eras and providing insights into cultural practices of the past.

The "Assassin's Creed" series is a prime example of how video games incorporate cultural heritage into their design. Each installment explores different historical settings, such as Renaissance Italy, ancient Egypt, and feudal Japan. The developers' dedication to historical accuracy and extensive research results in beautifully realized virtual worlds that immerse players in diverse cultures and time periods.

Moreover, cultural heritage can be celebrated in more contemporary settings as well. Games like "Cuphead" and "Hollow Knight" draw inspiration from vintage animation styles and classic platformers, celebrating the cultural heritage of animation and gaming history. These games pay homage to the art forms that laid the groundwork for modern gaming while introducing them to new generations.

Additionally, traditional music and art styles often find their way into video game soundtracks and visuals. Games like "Journey" use emotive musical compositions inspired by diverse cultural traditions to enhance the gaming experience and evoke a sense of cultural resonance.

By incorporating cultural heritage into their narratives, video games not only educate players about history and traditions but also foster a sense of cultural pride and identity. Players who explore these virtual worlds gain a deeper appreciation for the richness of human culture and the importance of preserving our collective heritage.

In conclusion, video games serve as vital tools for cultural preservation, reviving folklore, myths, and historical heritage for modern audiences. By drawing inspiration from diverse cultural sources, video games celebrate human storytelling and promote appreciation for different traditions. As gaming technology continues to advance, video games have the potential to become even more powerful vehicles for preserving cultural heritage and transmitting it to future generations. It is through these interactive experiences that gaming contributes to the ongoing preservation of human cultural legacy.

CHAPTER IV
The Educational Potential of Video Games

A. Gamification in Learning

Video games have the potential to revolutionize education by infusing elements of gaming into traditional learning processes. This section explores the concept of gamification in education, where game mechanics and design are employed to enhance student engagement, motivation, and learning outcomes. By integrating gamified educational platforms and promoting learning through gameplay, educators can harness the power of video games to create dynamic and effective learning experiences.

1. Gamified Educational Platforms:

Gamified educational platforms are online learning environments that incorporate game-like elements to motivate and reward students as they progress through educational content. These platforms often use points, badges, leaderboards, and other game mechanics to transform learning into an interactive and rewarding experience.

One notable example of a gamified educational platform is "Kahoot!" This platform allows teachers to create interactive quizzes and surveys that students can answer using their devices. The platform awards points for correct answers and displays a leaderboard to fuel friendly competition among students. "Kahoot!" promotes active participation, encourages critical thinking, and turns mundane quizzes into engaging experiences.

Another popular gamified learning tool is Duolingo, which teaches languages through bite-sized lessons, challenges, and achievements. The platform uses a leveling system and in-game rewards to keep learners motivated and committed to their language learning journey. Duolingo demonstrates how gamification can transform the acquisition of complex skills into enjoyable and accessible experiences.

By incorporating gamified elements, these platforms tap into the intrinsic motivation that games often generate. Students are driven to complete challenges, earn rewards, and progress through levels, fostering a sense of accomplishment and satisfaction in their learning journey.

2. Learning Through Gameplay:

Learning through gameplay involves integrating educational content and objectives directly into video games. This approach leverages the inherent interactivity and problem-solving aspects of games to deliver educational content in a captivating and memorable manner.

"Minecraft: Education Edition" exemplifies the potential of learning through gameplay. This educational version of the popular sandbox game allows students to explore historical settings, experiment with science concepts, and engage in collaborative building projects. By leveraging the creativity and open-ended nature of "Minecraft," educators can foster critical thinking, teamwork, and creativity while aligning with curricular objectives.

Educational games like "Osmo" and "Prodigy" also incorporate math, language, and other subject matter into the gameplay experience. These games present educational challenges and quests in an interactive format, encouraging students to solve problems, apply concepts, and receive immediate feedback on their progress.

The advantage of learning through gameplay is that it provides hands-on experiences that make learning more relatable and engaging. Instead of passive consumption of information, students actively participate in the learning process, which enhances retention and understanding.

Moreover, video games can immerse students in realistic simulations that allow them to apply theoretical knowledge in practical scenarios. For example, flight simulators can be used to train pilots, medical simulations prepare healthcare professionals, and city-building games offer insights into urban planning and management.

However, it is essential to ensure that educational games are designed effectively, aligning with educational goals and adhering to curriculum standards. Well-designed games strike a balance between educational content and entertaining gameplay, avoiding the risk of sacrificing learning objectives for mere amusement.

In conclusion, gamification in education and learning through gameplay are powerful tools that tap into the inherent motivational aspects of video games. Gamified educational platforms infuse learning with interactivity and rewards, promoting active engagement and knowledge retention. Learning through gameplay seamlessly integrates educational content into video games, creating immersive and experiential learning experiences. By embracing the educational potential of video games, educators can meet students' diverse learning needs while fostering a love for learning that transcends traditional classroom boundaries. As technology and game design continue to advance, the educational landscape is poised for further transformation through the creative fusion of gaming and learning.

B. Video Games in the Classroom

As technology advances and education evolves, video games are finding their way into the classroom as valuable tools for learning. This section explores the use of video games in educational settings, particularly focusing on serious games for education. It also delves into the challenges and benefits associated with integrating video games into traditional classrooms.

1. Serious Games for Education:

Serious games are video games explicitly designed for educational purposes, aiming to teach specific concepts or skills while engaging players in interactive gameplay. These games address a wide range of subjects, from mathematics and science to history and language arts, making them versatile tools for educators to reinforce learning objectives.

For instance, "Math Blaster" is a classic serious game that teaches math skills through arcade-style gameplay. Players solve math problems and puzzles to advance through levels, earning rewards and achievements along the way. By presenting math challenges in an engaging format, "Math Blaster" promotes active learning and problem-solving skills.

Similarly, "Foldit" is a serious game that allows players to explore protein folding and molecular structures. Players participate in scientific research by solving puzzles related to protein folding, contributing to real-world scientific discoveries. "Foldit" exemplifies how serious games can bridge the gap between education and scientific exploration, empowering students to make meaningful contributions to the scientific community.

Educators are increasingly using serious games as supplemental tools to reinforce classroom concepts, assess student progress, and provide personalized learning experiences. These games cater to different learning styles and allow students to learn at their own pace, creating a more inclusive and engaging learning environment.

2. Challenges and Benefits:

Integrating video games into the classroom presents both challenges and benefits for educators and students alike.

Challenges:

a. Curriculum Alignment: Ensuring that video games align with educational standards and learning objectives can be a challenge. Educators must carefully select games that complement their curricula and reinforce essential concepts.

b. Technical Infrastructure: Some educational games require specific technology or hardware, which may not be readily available in all classrooms. Schools must invest in the necessary infrastructure to support gaming experiences.

c. Teacher Training: Integrating video games effectively into the classroom requires teacher training and professional development. Educators need to understand how to use these tools to facilitate learning and maximize their impact.

d. Screen Time Management: Balancing screen time with other educational activities is essential to maintain a healthy learning environment. Overreliance on video games can hinder real-world interactions and other forms of learning.

Benefits:

a. Engagement and Motivation: Video games inherently offer an engaging and motivating learning experience. When students are actively involved in interactive gameplay, they are more likely to stay focused and committed to the learning process.

b. Differentiation and Personalization: Video games can adapt to individual learner needs, providing personalized challenges and feedback. This adaptability supports differentiated instruction, catering to diverse learning styles and abilities.

c. Critical Thinking and Problem-Solving: Many educational games require critical thinking and problem-solving skills. Students learn to analyze situations, make decisions, and strategize to progress in the game.

d. Collaboration and Communication: Multiplayer games promote collaboration and communication among students. They must work together, discuss strategies, and share ideas to achieve shared objectives.

e. Immediate Feedback: Educational games often provide immediate feedback, allowing students to assess their progress and identify areas for improvement in real-time.

In conclusion, video games have become valuable assets in modern classrooms, offering educational potential through serious games designed explicitly for learning purposes. These games engage students in interactive experiences that reinforce learning objectives and foster critical thinking and problem-solving skills. While challenges such as curriculum alignment and technical infrastructure exist, the benefits of integrating video games into the classroom are significant, including increased student engagement, personalization of learning experiences, and the cultivation of essential skills. With thoughtful implementation and teacher training, video games can continue to enhance education, transforming traditional classrooms into dynamic and inclusive learning environments that cater to the diverse needs of today's learners.

C. Video Games and Cognitive Development

Video games have been recognized for their potential to positively impact cognitive development, fostering essential skills that extend beyond the realm of gaming. This section explores how video games contribute to the development of problem-solving skills and spatial awareness, while also enhancing memory retention. By engaging in interactive gameplay, players can exercise their minds and cultivate cognitive abilities that have practical applications in various aspects of life.

1. Problem-Solving Skills:

Problem-solving is a fundamental cognitive skill that empowers individuals to analyze challenges, devise strategies, and reach effective solutions. Video games, especially puzzle-solving and strategy games, provide an ideal platform for honing these skills in a dynamic and engaging manner.

Puzzle games like "Portal" and "Tetris" require players to think critically and devise creative solutions to progress through levels. Players must analyze the environment, anticipate consequences, and experiment with different approaches to overcome obstacles. These games encourage a trial-and-error approach, teaching players to persevere and adapt their strategies as they encounter new challenges.

Strategy games, such as "Civilization" and "Age of Empires," foster long-term planning and decision-making skills. Players must manage resources, plan military campaigns, and navigate complex diplomatic situations. These games cultivate strategic thinking and encourage players to consider both short-term and long-term consequences of their actions.

Moreover, the problem-solving skills developed through gaming can transfer to real-world situations. Individuals who engage in complex and challenging games often exhibit better problem-solving abilities in academic, professional, and personal settings. The ability to approach problems analytically and develop effective solutions is a valuable skill in various domains of life.

2. Spatial Awareness and Memory:

Spatial awareness and memory are crucial cognitive skills that enable individuals to navigate their physical environment, retain information, and recall past experiences. Video games, particularly those with immersive 3D environments, can significantly impact the development of these skills.

Games like "Minecraft" and "Super Mario 3D World" require players to navigate intricate landscapes, coordinating precise movements and spatial reasoning. These experiences enhance players' spatial awareness and motor skills, as they learn to understand and manipulate virtual spaces.

Memory is also heavily engaged during gameplay. Players must remember game rules, patterns, and specific sequences to progress and succeed. Games that incorporate complex narratives, such as role-playing games (RPGs) and adventure games, challenge players to retain vast amounts of information, characters, and plotlines. This exercise of memory contributes to enhanced memory retention and recall abilities.

Additionally, some video games explicitly target memory improvement through brain-training exercises. "Brain Age" and "Lumosity" are examples of games that provide activities designed to challenge memory and other cognitive functions. While research on the long-term effectiveness of these games is still evolving, they highlight the potential for video games to serve as cognitive training tools.

Beyond gaming, the spatial awareness and memory developed through video games have real-world applications. Spatial awareness aids in activities like navigation, driving, and sports, while improved memory enhances academic performance and everyday tasks like remembering appointments and to-do lists.

In conclusion, video games offer substantial cognitive benefits, contributing to the development of problem-solving skills, spatial awareness, and memory retention. Puzzle and strategy games cultivate critical thinking and strategic planning, while immersive environments enhance spatial awareness and motor skills. The engagement of memory in gameplay improves retention and recall abilities. As these cognitive skills have broad applications in various aspects of life, the educational potential of video games extends beyond the realm of entertainment. Embracing gaming as a tool for cognitive development can empower individuals of all ages to enhance their problem-solving abilities, spatial awareness, and memory retention, enriching their cognitive capabilities and overall quality of life.

CHAPTER V
Video Games and Mental Health

A. The Psychology of Gaming

Video games have a profound impact on mental health, influencing emotions, behaviors, and overall well-being. This section delves into the psychology of gaming, examining how video games can serve as both a form of escapism that enhances psychological well-being and a potential trigger for gaming addiction and compulsive behavior.

1. Escapism and Psychological Well-being:

One of the most notable psychological aspects of gaming is its role as a form of escapism. Video games offer immersive experiences and captivating virtual worlds that allow players to temporarily disconnect from the stresses of real life. This aspect of gaming can positively impact mental health by providing relief from anxiety, depression, and everyday worries.

For individuals experiencing stress or emotional challenges, engaging in a captivating video game can serve as a healthy coping mechanism. The sense of control and achievement that comes with overcoming challenges in games can boost self-esteem and confidence. Moreover, gaming provides an opportunity for social connection, allowing players to form bonds with other gamers and combat feelings of loneliness.

Furthermore, video games often evoke emotions such as joy, excitement, and awe. The emotional engagement of gaming can be therapeutic, enhancing positive affect and promoting a sense of happiness and well-being.

Research has shown that certain video games designed to promote relaxation and mindfulness, such as "Journey" and "Flower," can reduce stress and anxiety. These games focus on calming visuals, soothing music, and peaceful environments, providing players with a meditative experience.

However, while gaming can offer psychological benefits as a form of escapism, it is essential to strike a balance and ensure that gaming does not become a maladaptive coping mechanism or lead to problematic gaming behaviors.

2. Gaming Addiction and Compulsive Behavior:

Despite the positive aspects of gaming, excessive and uncontrolled gaming can lead to gaming addiction and compulsive behavior. Gaming addiction, also known as Internet Gaming Disorder (IGD), is a behavioral addiction characterized by an excessive and uncontrollable urge to play video games.

Individuals with gaming addiction may neglect other responsibilities, such as school, work, or social relationships, in favor of gaming. They may experience withdrawal symptoms, such as irritability and restlessness, when unable to play. Over time, gaming addiction can have adverse effects on mental health, leading to feelings of guilt, depression, and anxiety.

Moreover, certain game design elements, such as reward systems and loot boxes, can trigger compulsive behaviors. The unpredictable nature of rewards in some games can lead to a "variable reinforcement schedule," which is highly addictive and reinforces gaming behavior.

Recognizing gaming addiction and compulsive gaming behavior is essential for promoting mental health. Supportive interventions, such as cognitive-behavioral therapy (CBT), can help individuals develop healthier gaming habits and address any underlying emotional issues contributing to excessive gaming.

Game developers and industry stakeholders also play a role in promoting responsible gaming practices. Implementing mechanisms to limit gaming time and providing clear guidelines on responsible gaming can mitigate the risk of gaming addiction.

In conclusion, the psychology of gaming is complex, influencing mental health in various ways. As a form of escapism, video games can provide psychological well-being by offering relief from stress, fostering positive emotions, and promoting social connection. Mindful gaming experiences designed to promote relaxation can serve as therapeutic tools for reducing anxiety and stress.

However, excessive gaming and gaming addiction can have detrimental effects on mental health, leading to neglect of real-life responsibilities and contributing to negative emotions. Recognizing the potential risks of gaming addiction is crucial for promoting responsible gaming practices and fostering a healthy balance between gaming and other aspects of life. By understanding the psychology of gaming and its impact on mental health, individuals can harness the positive aspects of gaming for psychological well-being while mitigating potential risks associated with excessive and compulsive gaming behaviors.

B. Video Games as Therapeutic Tools

Video games have evolved beyond entertainment and are increasingly recognized as valuable therapeutic tools for improving mental health and well-being. This section explores the therapeutic applications of video games, examining how they are used in therapy and their effectiveness in managing stress and anxiety. By harnessing the power of gaming, mental health professionals can offer innovative and engaging interventions to support their clients' emotional and psychological needs.

1. Gaming in Therapy:

In recent years, mental health professionals have begun incorporating video games into therapeutic interventions to address a wide range of mental health issues. These games, known as "serious games" or "therapeutic games," are specifically designed to target psychological and emotional challenges.

One example is the use of virtual reality (VR) games in exposure therapy. VR technology allows therapists to create controlled environments in which clients can confront and manage anxiety-inducing situations. For individuals with phobias or post-traumatic stress disorder (PTSD), exposure therapy using VR can be an effective way to gradually desensitize them to triggering stimuli.

Additionally, video games are being used to support mental health treatment for conditions such as depression and anxiety. "SPARX," for instance, is a game developed to address depression in young people. The game uses cognitive-behavioral therapy (CBT) techniques, encouraging players to engage in positive thinking and problem-solving as they navigate the virtual world.

Gaming can also be integrated into talk therapy as a tool for enhancing communication and rapport between therapists and clients. Therapists might use cooperative multiplayer games as a means of fostering collaboration and encouraging clients to discuss their thoughts and feelings in a non-threatening context.

The interactive and engaging nature of video games offers a unique advantage in therapy, providing clients with a sense of agency and control over their experiences. This can help overcome resistance to treatment and make therapy more appealing and accessible to diverse populations.

2. Managing Stress and Anxiety:

Video games have shown promise in managing stress and anxiety, providing a healthy and enjoyable way to cope with emotional challenges. Games designed to promote relaxation, mindfulness, and stress reduction can serve as effective tools for self-care and emotional regulation.

"Flowy" games, such as "Journey" and "Abzu," offer calming experiences through serene visuals and tranquil soundscapes. These games allow players to immerse themselves in beautiful and peaceful environments, providing an opportunity for mindfulness and stress relief.

Similarly, puzzle games, such as "Sudoku" and "Tetris," can be mentally engaging and diverting, offering a brief respite from stress and anxious thoughts. These games require focus and concentration, redirecting attention away from stressors and promoting a sense of relaxation.

Mobile apps like "Headspace" and "Calm" incorporate gamified elements to teach meditation and deep-breathing exercises, encouraging users to incorporate mindfulness practices into their daily routines.

However, it is essential to use video games mindfully as a coping mechanism for stress and anxiety. While gaming can offer temporary relief, it should not replace other healthy coping strategies, such as exercise, social support, and professional help.

Moreover, some games, particularly those with intense or competitive gameplay, may increase stress levels for certain individuals. Individual preferences and emotional responses to specific game content must be taken into account when recommending games for stress management.

In conclusion, video games are emerging as powerful therapeutic tools for enhancing mental health and well-being. The use of serious games and virtual reality in therapy demonstrates the potential of gaming to address psychological challenges effectively. By integrating video games into therapeutic interventions, mental health professionals can engage clients in innovative and engaging treatments that empower them to manage their emotional and psychological needs.

Furthermore, gaming offers unique benefits for stress and anxiety management, providing an enjoyable and immersive escape from daily stressors. Relaxing and mindfulness-focused games can promote a sense of calm and emotional regulation, supporting self-care practices.

However, as with any therapeutic tool, the responsible and mindful use of video games is essential. Mental health professionals must carefully select games that align with their clients' needs and preferences, ensuring that gaming interventions complement and enhance traditional therapeutic approaches. By embracing the therapeutic potential of video games, mental health professionals can expand their toolkit and offer clients innovative and engaging interventions that promote mental health and well-being.

C. Addressing Concerns and Misconceptions

Video games have been a subject of concern and debate regarding their potential impact on mental health, particularly concerning violence and aggression. This section aims to address these concerns and misconceptions while highlighting the importance of balancing the benefits and risks of video game usage for mental well-being. Understanding the nuances of gaming's effects on mental health is essential for fostering informed discussions and responsible gaming practices.

1. Violence and Aggression in Games:

One of the most persistent concerns surrounding video games is the potential link between violent gameplay and real-life aggression. Some studies have suggested that exposure to violent video games may increase aggressive thoughts, feelings, and behaviors in certain individuals, particularly in the short term.

However, the relationship between video game violence and real-life aggression remains complex and nuanced. Research in this area has yielded mixed results, with some studies showing minimal or no significant long-term effects of violent gaming on aggression.

Furthermore, it is essential to recognize that many factors influence how individuals respond to video game content. Individual differences, family and social environments, and pre-existing aggressive tendencies all play significant roles in shaping a person's behavioral response to video games.

Moreover, the vast majority of players do not engage in aggressive or violent behaviors as a result of playing video games. The overwhelming majority of gamers can differentiate between fantasy and reality, understanding that actions in video games do not have real-world consequences.

Game developers and industry stakeholders also play a role in addressing concerns related to violence in games. Implementing age-appropriate content ratings and providing clear guidelines for parents can help ensure that young players are exposed to content suitable for their age and maturity level.

2. Balancing Benefits and Risks:

Like any form of media and entertainment, video games come with both benefits and risks. Understanding and balancing these aspects is essential for promoting responsible gaming practices and supporting mental well-being.

Benefits of Video Games:

- Cognitive Benefits: Video games can enhance problem-solving, spatial awareness, memory, and other cognitive skills, contributing to improved mental acuity.

- Emotional Well-being: Gaming can serve as a form of escapism, providing relief from stress, anxiety, and depression. It can also evoke positive emotions such as joy and excitement.

- Social Connection: Multiplayer and online gaming offer opportunities for social interaction and connection, fostering a sense of community among players.

- Educational Potential: Serious games can be valuable tools for learning and skill development, catering to diverse learning styles.

Risks of Video Games:

- Gaming Addiction: Excessive gaming can lead to gaming addiction, which may negatively impact academic, professional, and personal life.

- Sleep Disturbances: Prolonged gaming sessions, especially before bedtime, can disrupt sleep patterns, leading to sleep deprivation and related health issues.

- Sedentary Lifestyle: Extended periods of gaming can contribute to a sedentary lifestyle, which may have adverse effects on physical health.

Balancing the benefits and risks of video games requires mindful and responsible gaming practices. It is crucial for players, parents, educators, and mental health professionals to:

- Set limits on gaming time and encourage regular breaks to avoid excessive screen time.

- Choose age-appropriate games that align with individual interests and maturity levels.

- Encourage a healthy balance between gaming and other activities, such as physical exercise, social interactions, and academics.

- Stay informed about the content of video games and be proactive in addressing any concerns or potential negative effects.

- Be mindful of individual responses to gaming and be attentive to any signs of gaming addiction or negative behavioral changes.

In conclusion, addressing concerns and misconceptions about video games' impact on mental health is essential for fostering informed and responsible attitudes towards gaming. While violent video games have been a subject of concern, research indicates that the relationship between video game violence and real-life aggression is complex and influenced by multiple factors. It is essential to recognize the potential benefits of gaming, such as cognitive enhancement, emotional well-being, and social connection, while also acknowledging the risks, such as gaming addiction and sedentary behavior.

By promoting balanced and mindful gaming practices, individuals can enjoy the positive aspects of video games while minimizing potential negative effects. Open and informed discussions about video games and mental health can lead to greater understanding and responsible engagement with this evolving medium, benefiting players' overall well-being and mental health.

CHAPTER VI
The Future of Gaming: Technological and Social Trends

A. Virtual Reality and Augmented Reality

Advancements in technology are shaping the future of gaming, with virtual reality (VR) and augmented reality (AR) at the forefront of this transformation. This section explores the impact of VR and AR on gaming and beyond, while also delving into the social implications and ethical considerations surrounding these immersive technologies.

1. Impact on Gaming and Beyond:

Virtual Reality (VR): VR technology offers players a fully immersive and interactive experience, transporting them to virtual worlds where they can interact with the environment and objects in a natural way. The impact of VR on gaming is profound, elevating gameplay to new heights of realism and interactivity.

VR gaming experiences, such as "Half-Life: Alyx" and "Beat Saber," demonstrate the immense potential of the medium. Players can physically duck, dodge, and aim, fostering a sense of presence and embodiment within the game world. VR allows for innovative mechanics and gameplay design, revolutionizing traditional gaming genres and enabling entirely new experiences.

Beyond gaming, VR has diverse applications, including virtual tourism, training simulations, and therapeutic interventions. Medical professionals use VR to treat phobias and anxiety disorders, while industries like architecture and engineering utilize VR for virtual prototyping and visualization.

Augmented Reality (AR): AR overlays virtual elements onto the real world, blurring the boundary between the digital and physical realms. Popular examples of AR include "Pokémon GO" and "Minecraft Earth," which merge virtual content with real-world environments.

AR has transformative potential beyond gaming, particularly in fields such as education, retail, and navigation. In education, AR can enhance learning by providing interactive and visual aids, such as 3D models and historical reconstructions. In retail, AR allows customers to virtually try on clothes and visualize furniture in their homes before purchasing. AR navigation systems, like Google Maps' AR mode, guide users through cities with augmented directions.

As VR and AR technologies continue to advance, their integration into various sectors will drive innovation, enhancing user experiences and opening up new opportunities.

2. Social Implications and Ethical Considerations:

Social Interaction and Connectivity: VR and AR have significant implications for social interaction. VR allows for shared multiplayer experiences in virtual worlds, fostering a sense of presence and camaraderie among players. AR enhances real-life social interactions by providing additional information and context through virtual overlays.

While these technologies enable exciting social possibilities, it is essential to consider the potential consequences. Increased reliance on virtual interactions might impact face-to-face communication and lead to challenges related to privacy, safety, and cyberbullying within virtual spaces.

Ethical Considerations: VR and AR raise important ethical questions concerning data privacy, user consent, and digital ownership. As these technologies gather vast amounts of user data to enhance experiences and personalize content, safeguarding user privacy becomes critical. Transparent data policies and informed consent mechanisms are necessary to protect user rights.

Additionally, virtual assets and experiences in VR and AR hold value for users, prompting discussions about digital ownership and intellectual property rights. Developers and platform owners must navigate these complex issues to ensure fair and ethical practices.

Health and Well-being: Prolonged use of VR may lead to potential health concerns, including motion sickness and visual discomfort. Developers must prioritize user comfort and implement design features that minimize these effects. Moreover, excessive use of VR and AR can lead to the neglect of real-world responsibilities, emphasizing the need for responsible usage guidelines and user education.

Digital Divide: VR and AR technologies require specialized hardware and devices, leading to potential disparities in access and participation. Socioeconomic factors may affect an individual's ability to afford VR or AR equipment, creating a digital divide between those who can access these technologies and those who cannot. Addressing accessibility issues and promoting inclusive design is crucial to ensuring equitable access to immersive experiences.

In conclusion, the future of gaming is intertwined with the advancements in virtual reality (VR) and augmented reality (AR). VR enhances gaming experiences through full immersion and innovative gameplay mechanics, while AR overlays virtual content onto the real world, revolutionizing various industries. Beyond gaming, these technologies have far-reaching implications, impacting social interactions, education, retail, and navigation.

However, the adoption of VR and AR raises ethical considerations, including data privacy, digital ownership, and user consent. Developers and industry stakeholders must prioritize responsible practices to protect user rights and privacy. Additionally, addressing health and well-being concerns, such as motion sickness and digital addiction, is crucial to promoting safe and enjoyable experiences.

As VR and AR continue to shape the future of gaming and technology, it is essential to strike a balance between technological advancements and ethical considerations. By fostering inclusive, responsible, and user-centric development, the potential of VR and AR can be harnessed to enrich lives, enhance experiences, and create a more connected and immersive world.

B. Esports and Professional Gaming

Esports, or competitive video gaming, is a rapidly growing phenomenon that has transformed the landscape of the gaming industry and entertainment as a whole. This section explores the rise of competitive gaming, its influence on traditional sports, and its potential trajectory as a major player in the future of entertainment and sports.

1. Rise of Competitive Gaming:

Esports has experienced a meteoric rise in popularity and viewership over the past decade. What was once a niche activity confined to small gatherings of gaming enthusiasts has evolved into a global multimillion-dollar industry with a massive fan base.

The accessibility of online gaming platforms and live streaming services like Twitch and YouTube Gaming has been a major catalyst for the growth of esports. These platforms enable players to showcase their skills and personalities to a vast audience, transcending geographical boundaries.

Major esports events, such as The International (Dota 2), League of Legends World Championship, and Fortnite World Cup, draw millions of viewers and offer substantial prize pools. Esports tournaments attract players from around the world, and teams are backed by influential organizations and sponsors.

Esports athletes, often referred to as "professional gamers," are now recognized as legitimate athletes. They train rigorously, adhere to strict schedules, and compete in high-stakes tournaments, all while developing loyal fan bases.

Esports encompasses a wide range of game genres, including first-person shooters, real-time strategy, sports simulations, and fighting games. The diversity of games contributes to the broad appeal of esports, attracting fans from different gaming communities.

2. The Influence on Traditional Sports:

Esports' surge in popularity has caught the attention of traditional sports organizations and investors, leading to a growing convergence between the two domains.

Sports franchises and individual athletes have entered the esports arena by forming esports teams or investing in existing ones. Many professional sports leagues, including the NBA and NFL, have launched their own esports leagues to capitalize on the growing esports audience.

This crossover has brought new opportunities for esports athletes, as well as new revenue streams for traditional sports organizations. It has also facilitated the exchange of expertise between the two industries, leading to innovations in fan engagement and content creation.

Esports events are now filling major stadiums and arenas, drawing comparable crowds to traditional sports competitions. The live atmosphere at esports tournaments is electrifying, with fans cheering for their favorite teams and players.

Moreover, esports' digital nature has enabled unique opportunities for fan interaction and virtual experiences. Viewers can watch matches in real-time, participate in online chat rooms, and engage with their favorite players through social media platforms.

The rise of esports has also influenced traditional sports in terms of content distribution and engagement. Many sports leagues now offer online streaming of games and behind-the-scenes content, mirroring the esports industry's successful approach to online viewership.

The Future of Esports: As technology continues to evolve, the future of esports is filled with possibilities. VR and AR technologies may play a significant role in shaping the future of competitive gaming, creating even more immersive and interactive experiences for players and viewers.

Esports could also become a major contender in the Olympic Games and other global sporting events. The International Olympic Committee has acknowledged the growth and significance of esports and has started exploring potential partnerships.

The continued integration of esports into mainstream entertainment and sports culture will likely lead to further growth and expansion. Esports will continue to attract top talent, secure lucrative sponsorships, and appeal to a diverse and global audience.

However, with the increasing professionalization of esports, there are challenges to address, such as player well-being, mental health, and fair labor practices. It is essential for the industry to prioritize player welfare and establish supportive structures to safeguard athletes' physical and mental health.

In conclusion, esports has emerged as a dominant force in the future of gaming, entertainment, and sports. The rise of competitive gaming, with its massive fan base and global reach, has transformed how people engage with gaming and has paved the way for new opportunities for athletes and traditional sports organizations. Esports' influence extends beyond gaming, shaping content distribution and fan engagement strategies for traditional sports as well. The future of esports holds exciting potential for technological innovation, international recognition, and continued growth as a major entertainment industry. However, addressing the challenges of player well-being and creating sustainable and inclusive structures will be essential for ensuring the long-term success and positive impact of esports on the world stage.

C. Gaming and Social Change

Gaming has evolved into a powerful platform with the potential to drive social change and shape the future of society. This section explores the role of gaming in social movements and how it can influence broader societal trends, fostering positive impacts on individuals and communities.

1. Potential for Social Movements:

Video games have emerged as a means of raising awareness and promoting social causes. They provide unique opportunities for storytelling and immersive experiences that can evoke empathy and understanding among players.

Games like "That Dragon, Cancer" and "Papo & Yo" tackle sensitive topics such as cancer and domestic abuse, offering players a glimpse into the lived experiences of individuals facing adversity. By conveying these narratives through interactive gameplay, these games foster emotional connections and encourage players to reflect on important social issues.

Moreover, gaming communities have become hubs for charitable initiatives and social activism. Many gamers participate in events like "Extra Life" and "Games Done Quick," where they raise funds for charities by streaming gaming sessions. These initiatives demonstrate the power of gaming to unite people worldwide in support of worthy causes.

Additionally, virtual worlds within massive multiplayer online games (MMOs) have been utilized to host rallies and protests, creating virtual spaces for advocacy and social change. Players from different backgrounds come together in these virtual realms to amplify their voices and draw attention to various global issues.

The potential for social movements within gaming extends beyond the games themselves. Esports events, with their massive viewership and international reach, offer an opportunity to spread messages of inclusivity, equality, and positive change to a vast global audience.

2. Shaping the Future of Society:

As gaming continues to permeate popular culture, it is increasingly influencing broader societal trends and behaviors. This influence extends to various aspects of life, including education, health, and the workplace.

Education: Gaming has the potential to revolutionize education by offering interactive and engaging learning experiences. Serious games and educational platforms incorporate gaming elements to teach complex concepts in a fun and interactive manner. These games cater to diverse learning styles and promote active participation, resulting in improved retention and understanding of academic material.

Health: Gaming is making significant strides in the health sector. Virtual reality is used in medical training, surgical simulations, and pain management therapies. Gamification elements are incorporated into healthcare apps to encourage healthy habits and support patient compliance with treatment plans.

Workplace: The gamification of workplaces is becoming more prevalent, with companies using game-like elements to incentivize employee productivity and engagement. Gamified training programs encourage skill development and foster a culture of continuous learning within organizations.

Furthermore, gaming communities have become spaces for social interaction, support, and friendship. The sense of belonging and camaraderie within these communities can combat feelings of isolation and loneliness, benefiting mental well-being.

Gaming's impact on society is not without challenges. Concerns related to online toxicity, cyberbullying, and addictive behaviors must be addressed through responsible gaming practices and community moderation. Developers, platforms, and gamers alike play a role in creating inclusive, safe, and supportive gaming environments.

The Future of Gaming and Social Change: The future of gaming as a catalyst for social change is promising. As technology continues to evolve, gaming experiences will become more immersive, allowing players to connect emotionally with characters and stories. This emotional resonance can lead to increased empathy and understanding of diverse perspectives.

The accessibility of gaming across different devices and platforms will also contribute to its potential for social impact. Gaming's universal appeal transcends age, gender, and cultural boundaries, making it a powerful tool for reaching a diverse audience.

Gaming's integration with virtual reality and augmented reality technologies will further expand its capacity to promote social change. VR experiences can create heightened levels of presence and emotional engagement, enabling players to step into the shoes of others and experience complex social issues firsthand.

In conclusion, gaming holds tremendous potential to drive social change and shape the future of society. Through interactive storytelling, charitable initiatives, and social activism within gaming communities, the medium has proven its capacity to raise awareness of important social issues. Moreover, gaming's influence extends to education, health, and the workplace, transforming these domains and enhancing individual experiences.

As gaming continues to evolve, its impact on social change will likely become even more profound. The future of gaming holds exciting possibilities, with VR and AR technologies offering immersive and transformative experiences. Embracing responsible gaming practices, fostering inclusive communities, and utilizing gaming for positive social purposes will be essential for harnessing the full potential of gaming as a force for positive change in society.

Conclusion

A. Recapitulation of Key Findings

The exploration of "Gaming Beyond Entertainment: The Social and Cultural Impact of Video Games" has unveiled a dynamic and multi-faceted landscape that extends far beyond mere entertainment. From the rise of video games to their cultural and educational implications, as well as their impact on mental health and the future of society, video games have proven to be a significant force in shaping our world. Let us recapitulate the key findings of this book.

I. Introduction: In the introduction, we set the stage for understanding the broader impact of video games. We highlighted the rise of video games from simple entertainment to a powerful social and cultural phenomenon that influences various aspects of modern life.

II. Exploring the Social Impact of Video Games: Under this section, we explored how video games have become social platforms, fostering online gaming communities and virtual reality experiences. Additionally, we examined how video games contribute to social skills development, promoting communication, teamwork, empathy, and emotional intelligence. We also investigated the relationship between video games and social issues, including representation and diversity, as well as the emergence of gaming as a platform for social activism.

III. Investigating the Cultural Influence of Video Games: In this section, we delved into video games as cultural artifacts, examining their role in expressing ideas and storytelling traditions. We also analyzed the representation of cultural stereotypes in video games, exploring their impact on global perceptions and the importance of responsible representation. Lastly, we explored how video games contribute to cultural preservation, reviving folklore, myths, and heritage in gaming experiences.

IV. The Educational Potential of Video Games: Under this section, we explored how video games are increasingly used in education, promoting gamification in learning and offering gamified educational platforms. We also discussed the integration of video games in the classroom through serious games and their challenges and benefits. Moreover, we investigated the positive impact of video games on cognitive development, particularly problem-solving skills, spatial awareness, and memory.

V. Video Games and Mental Health: This section shed light on the psychology of gaming, showcasing how video games can serve as a form of escapism, positively impacting psychological well-being. We also addressed gaming addiction and compulsive behaviors, emphasizing the importance of responsible gaming practices. Additionally, we explored how video games can be utilized as therapeutic tools for managing stress, anxiety, and even psychological treatment through virtual reality.

VI. The Future of Gaming: Technological and Social Trends: In this section, we explored the rise of esports and professional gaming, which have transformed gaming into a global industry with a massive fan base. Esports' influence on traditional sports and content distribution is evident, showcasing the potential for further growth and convergence between gaming and sports. Moreover, we discussed gaming's potential as a platform for social change, fostering social movements and shaping the future of society through immersive experiences and meaningful narratives.

VII. Conclusion: The journey through the social and cultural impact of video games has been a fascinating one. Video games have transcended their early origins to become a powerful and influential medium that shapes society, educates, entertains, and fosters social change. From the positive effects on cognitive development and social skills to their potential as therapeutic tools, video games offer far-reaching benefits to individuals and communities alike.

However, it is crucial to recognize the challenges and responsibilities that come with gaming's rise to prominence. Responsible gaming practices, ethical considerations, and inclusivity should be at the forefront as the gaming industry continues to evolve.

In conclusion, "Gaming Beyond Entertainment: The Social and Cultural Impact of Video Games" invites us to reflect on the transformative power of this medium and its potential to inspire positive change in the world. As technology advances and gaming continues to shape our society, it is essential for stakeholders, developers, players, and educators to embrace this potential responsibly and ensure that gaming remains a force for good in our ever-evolving world.

B. Reflection on the Evolving Gaming Landscape

As we conclude our exploration of "Gaming Beyond Entertainment: The Social and Cultural Impact of Video Games," it is essential to reflect on the ever-evolving gaming landscape and the profound changes it has brought to our world. From its humble beginnings as a form of entertainment to its current status as a powerful platform for education, social interaction, and social change, gaming has journeyed far beyond what anyone could have envisioned.

The gaming industry's transformation from a niche hobby to a global cultural phenomenon is a testament to the power of innovation and technological advancement. The rise of virtual reality, augmented reality, and esports has opened new frontiers, expanding gaming's reach and influence to unprecedented heights.

Moreover, the cultural and social impact of video games has been profound. Gaming has become a medium for expression, storytelling, and the preservation of cultural heritage. It has challenged stereotypes and opened up dialogues about representation and diversity in media. Through social platforms and online communities, gaming has brought people together, transcending geographical boundaries and fostering connections between individuals with shared interests.

One of the most striking developments in the gaming landscape is its educational potential. Video games have proven to be effective tools for learning, promoting problem-solving, critical thinking, and creativity. Gamified educational platforms offer a dynamic and engaging approach to teaching, catering to diverse learning styles and preferences. The integration of gaming in the classroom has the potential to revolutionize traditional education and inspire a new generation of learners.

C. Envisioning a Balanced Gaming Future

As we look to the future of gaming, it is essential to envision a balanced approach that maximizes the positive impact of gaming while mitigating potential challenges. Responsible gaming practices must be at the forefront, ensuring that gaming remains a healthy and enriching activity for players of all ages.

1. Prioritizing Player Well-being: The well-being of players must be a primary consideration for developers and stakeholders. Measures should be in place to address gaming addiction, excessive screen time, and potential health issues. Game design should promote moderation and incorporate features that encourage breaks and physical activity.

2. Emphasizing Inclusivity and Diversity: The gaming industry should continue to work towards greater inclusivity and representation. Diverse voices should be amplified, both in game development and in the narratives depicted in games. Ensuring that games reflect the richness and diversity of our global community can create a more inclusive and empathetic gaming experience.

3. Cultivating Positive Online Communities: Online toxicity and harassment remain significant challenges in gaming. Developers and platforms must take proactive steps to foster positive and safe online environments. Community moderation and reporting systems should be robust, enabling players to engage in healthy and respectful interactions.

4. Embracing Ethical Game Design: Ethical considerations in game design are crucial. Games should avoid promoting harmful behaviors or perpetuating negative stereotypes. Instead, they should encourage positive values, empathy, and critical thinking.

5. Expanding Gaming for Social Change: Gaming's potential as a platform for social change should be harnessed further. Developers can continue to create games that raise awareness about social issues and inspire players to take action in real-life contexts. Esports events can be utilized to promote inclusivity, equality, and global cooperation.

6. Engaging in Lifelong Learning: The future of gaming is closely tied to technological advancements. Players, developers, and educators must be open to lifelong learning to stay abreast of emerging trends and opportunities. Embracing new technologies and innovation will ensure that gaming remains relevant and impactful.

In conclusion, "Gaming Beyond Entertainment: The Social and Cultural Impact of Video Games" has provided us with a comprehensive understanding of the multifaceted world of gaming. From its impact on education, culture, and mental health to its potential for social change, gaming has demonstrated its ability to shape the future of society positively. Envisioning a balanced gaming future requires a collaborative effort from all stakeholders, including developers, players, educators, and policymakers. By embracing responsible practices, promoting inclusivity, and harnessing the transformative power of gaming, we can create a gaming landscape that continues to inspire, educate, and unite people worldwide. The future of gaming is filled with potential, and it is our collective responsibility to ensure that it remains a force for good in our rapidly changing world.